TEXAS CHRISTMAS

As Celebrated Under Six Flags

SPAIN

FRANCE

MEXICO

TEXAS

CONFEDERACY

UNITED STATES

By Elizabeth Dearing Morgan

EAKIN PRESS ⬦ Austin, Texas

Library of Congress Cataloging-in-Publication Data

Morgan, Elizabeth Dearing. (1960–)
    Texas Christmas : as celebrated under six flags / by Elizabeth Dearing
Morgan. — 1st. ed.
        p.   cm.
    Includes bibliographical references and index.
    Summary: Describes some of the different ways that Christmas has been
celebrated by various groups in Texas from the sixteenth century to the
present.
    ISBN 1-57168-067-5
    1. Christmas — Texas — History — Juvenile literature. 2. Texas — Social
life and customs — Juvenile literature. [1. Christmas — Texas. 2. Texas —
Social life and customs.] I. Title.
    GT 4986.T4M67   1996
    394.2'663'09764--dc20   95-35770
                                                                          CIP
                                                                           AC

Cover illustration by Mark Mitchell

For my son,
Clinton Lee Morgan

my nephews,
Jason Louis Johnson
Justin William Johnson
Travis Wayne Dearing

and my niece,
Ericka Christine Price.

Contents

Chapter 1

The Christmas Story

Christmas celebrates the birth of Jesus Christ on December 25 of each year. The story of Christmas is told in the Books of Saint Matthew and Saint Luke in the New Testament of the Holy Bible. It begins when God sent the angel Gabriel to a city called Nazareth. (This city is now in the country of Israel.) There Gabriel spoke to a young woman named Mary. Gabriel told her that she was blessed by God and would have a son named Jesus. The child would be called the Son of God.

An angel also went to a man named Joseph, who was going to be the husband of Mary. The angel told Joseph not to fear getting married to Mary, because her baby was made from the Holy Ghost.

When it was time for Mary to have the baby, she and Joseph had to go to the city of Bethlehem (Israel) to pay a tax. They had to sleep in a barn because there was no room for them at the inn.

While they were there, Mary gave birth to Baby Jesus. She wrapped him in swaddling clothes (long, narrow strips of cloth that were used long ago to keep a baby

1

from moving very much). She laid him in a manger, which is a trough where cattle eat.

That night some shepherds were watching over their flock. An angel came and told them their Saviour, Christ the Lord, was born. Then a group of angels said, "Glory to God in the highest, and on earth peace, good will toward men." The shepherds went to see Baby Jesus.

Three Wise Men from the east followed a star to come and worship Baby Jesus. This guiding light came to be known as the Star of Bethlehem. The Wise Men brought treasured gifts and gave Baby Jesus gold, and frankincense (pure incense to burn in church), and myrrh (perfume).

Jesus grew up and performed many miracles. Some priests and other people didn't believe he was the Son of God. They felt it was a sin for him to say he was. So Jesus was nailed to a cross as punishment. The priests said if Jesus was truly the Son of God, then he would have the power to escape from the cross. If he did that, they would believe that he was the Son of God.

Jesus died on the cross. But three days later, he rose from the dead. He continued to perform miracles and gained many believers.

In the Christian religion, Jesus Christ is considered the most important person in the history of the world. In fact, recorded time for most of the world begins with his birth. The years before Jesus Christ was born are called "B.C.," which stands for "Before Christ." The years after his birth are called "A.D.," which stands for *"Anno Domini."* This is Latin for "in the Year of Our Lord." Whatever the current year is, it has been that many years since Christ was born.

The Christian religion has more than one billion followers around the world. This is more than any other religion. The Christian religion includes the Protestant church, the Roman Catholic church, and the Eastern Orthodox church.

The Protestant church is divided into different churches: Baptist, Methodist, Lutheran, Church of Christ, and many others. Protestants are the largest of the three groups in America. The Catholic church runs a very close second in number of followers. There are not as many members of the Eastern Orthodox religion. Most who are members of this religion belong to the Greek Orthodox church.

The largest group of non-Christians in Texas, the Jews, celebrate Hanukkah near Christmastime. Hanukkah is known as the Festival of Lights because the Jews light a candle every night for eight nights. They light a *menorah* (a candlestick) to celebrate the time when the Jewish people recovered their temple in Jerusalem from the Syrians in the days before Christ. The candles also symbolize the miracle that although the Jews only had enough lamp oil to last one night, their Eternal Lamp burned for eight.

The many branches of the Christian religion may differ in some ways. But they all share in the delight of celebrating the birth of Jesus Christ at Christmastime. In Texas, Christmas has been celebrated in many different ways because of the state's long and varied history.

Chapter 2

Christmas When Spain Ruled Texas, 1519–1685

The first people to live in Texas, the Native Americans, didn't celebrate Christmas because they weren't Christians. The first Christians who came to Texas were from Spain.

The Spanish explorers who landed in Texas in 1519 were Catholic, and they brought the idea of Christmas with them. They celebrated Christmas with religious services. Christmas means "Christ's mass." Mass is the main religious service of worship in the Roman Catholic church.

The first recorded Texas Christmas celebration was in 1599. The Spanish ladies and gentlemen had a Christmas pageant near El Paso. Indians who lived in the area helped them act out the journey of the Three Wise Men to Bethlehem.

The tradition of the *piñata* dates back to this period as well. The explorers brought the game from Spain. A papier-mâche figure is decorated with crepe paper and filled with candies and tiny toys. The figure may be in the shape of an animal, a star, Santa Claus, or any other holiday symbol.

The *piñata* is hung from a rope. Then players are blindfolded and take turns swinging at the *piñata* with a stick. Eventually the *piñata* is cracked open, and the candies come pouring down. Everyone grabs up their share of goodies.

Another early Texas Christmas was described in 1683, when Spanish soldiers camped on the Rio Grande. On Christmas Day they said a mass and planted a holy cross.

A couple of years later, the Spanish lost their 166-year hold on Texas for a short time.

A young Texan visits with the French Santa Claus, Père Noël, *at the Christmas at the French Legation celebration in Austin.*
— Photo by Elizabeth Dearing Morgan

6

Chapter 3

Christmas When France Ruled Texas, 1685–1690

France ruled Texas for only five years, long ago. The French were led to Texas by an explorer named La Salle. He set up a colony called Fort Saint Louis. The people from France were Catholics, like the people from Spain. But, of course, they spoke French instead of Spanish.

In 1686 the French colonists sang a Midnight Mass for Christmas. They also celebrated Epiphany. Epiphany is held on January 6 to remember the day that the Three Wise Men came to honor Baby Jesus at Bethlehem. Epiphany is also called Twelfth-Day, because it happens twelve days after Christmas. Epiphany, or Twelfth-Day, marks the end of the Christmas season.

To celebrate Twelfth-Day in 1686, the French explorers followed their custom. They drank a toast to their king back in France. They cried, "The king drinks!" But they had run out of brandy. All they had for the toast was water.

French rule did not last long. La Salle was murdered and the colony was abandoned. Spain once again took control of Texas.

French people did not come to Texas in large numbers again for almost 150 years. During the days of the Republic of Texas, the French Legation was built in Austin. It served as the home and office of the French diplomat to the Republic of Texas.

Today the French Legation is owned by the Daughters of the Republic of Texas. This is an organization of women whose ancestors lived in Texas when Texas was its own nation. Every year in December they sponsor an event called Christmas at the French Legation.

Christmas at the French Legation allows visitors to relive the year 1841 and take a tour of the house, kitchen, and carriage house. Actors and tour guides wear costumes from those early days. The French version of Santa Claus, *"Père Noël,"* appears in a carriage. Refreshments are served, and there is a Christmas bazaar selling handmade Texas items and herbs from the French Legation's garden. The money raised is used to keep the buildings in good shape.

Today in Texas there are two main areas where French Texans live. One is Castroville, which was settled by a group of French people during the 1840s. The other is along the border with southern Louisiana around Beaumont, Port Arthur, and Orange. This is where French Cajuns live. Cajuns are the descendants of French people who moved to Canada and then to Louisiana. Christmas celebrations in these two areas have a French flavor. There you may hear *"Joyeux Noël!"* which is French for "Joyous Christmas!"

Christmas trees are very important to French Texans. They decorate them with homemade cookies. The cookies have taken the place of communion wafers to symbolize the body of Christ.

French Texans call the Nativity scene a *"crèche."* These *crèches* are another important part of Christmas to French Texans.

French cooking is famous around the world. French Texans like to serve a *"buche de Noël,"* or Christmas Cake, with Christmas dinner. It is a chocolate cake rolled up to look like a yule log. It is often served with spiced coffee.

French Texans keep the holiday spirit until Epiphany. Since the Three Wise Men are also known as the Three Kings, the French call Epiphany "the Feast of the Kings." They celebrate with parties.

Chapter 4

Christmas When Spain Again Ruled Texas, 1690–1821

When the French colony at Fort Saint Louis failed, Spain once again ruled Texas, for the next 131 years. They began building quite a few missions. In the 1700s, priests lived at the missions and tried to teach the Indians to become Christians. The Spanish priests found that the Apaches also worshiped the son of the creator.

At Christmastime the Spanish priests and the Indians celebrated together. The priests held masses, marches, feasts, and festivals to tell the Indians about the birth of Christ. The Indians did matachinas dances to show the struggle between good and evil.

In 1731 a group of people from the Canary Islands moved to San Antonio. These Spanish-speaking people brought with them a custom called *"Las Posadas,"* which means "The Inns."

For *Las Posadas,* groups of families act out Mary and Joseph's search for an inn. They sing Christmas carols and go from one house to the next and are turned away. Finally, someone lets them in. They pray in front of a *nacimiento,* which is Spanish for Nativity scene, and celebrate with a party and a *piñata.*

Every year the San Antonio Conservation Society sponsors a *Las Posadas.* The whole city can participate in the event, which takes place along the River Walk. Stops are made at the beautiful hotels along the way. Finally, the participants find their way to a celebration featuring *piñatas,* dancing, and snacks.

A few decades later, another Spanish custom was brought to Texas. In 1776, a play called *"Los Pastores"* was performed at Mission San José in San Antonio. *"Los Pastores"* is Spanish for "The Shepherds." The play is still performed at Mission San José. Like *Las Posadas,* it is sponsored by the San Antonio Conservation Society.

The long play is about the shepherds as they try to get

This is the cast of "Los Pastores" *that performed the play in San Antonio during Christmas of 1893.*
— Photo courtesy University of Texas Institute of Texan Cultures, San Antonio, Texas

to Bethlehem to see Baby Jesus. The play is free and the audience can buy food and drinks to enjoy while watching.

An old Spanish custom that became popular in Texas in the 1700s is the lighting of *luminarias,* or "little fires." In Spain the tradition of lighting *luminarias* has been around for many years. The little bonfires represent the ones that the shepherds who went to see Baby Jesus would build for warmth and protection.

The Spanish Texans lit little bonfires at Christmastime for many symbolic reasons. Some say the light helps Mary and Joseph find their way to Bethlehem. Some say it helps the Three Wise Men or even Baby Jesus find their way.

During Spanish rule, Americans brought brown paper sacks to Texas for the first time. Instead of making little bonfires from tree branches, Texans started placing candles in a bed of sand inside the sacks. Today there are even ceramic or plastic holders that look like paper sacks, with electric light bulbs inside. The towns of El Paso and San Antonio are well known for their displays of *luminarias.*

By 1810, more and more Spanish people had come to live in Texas. In San Antonio they celebrated Christmas with bullfights and bazaar booths.

In 1821, the people of Mexico won their freedom from Spain in a war called the Mexican Revolution. Mexico became its own country, and it took over control of Texas.

Chapter 5

Christmas When Mexico Ruled Texas, 1821–1836

Mexico owned Texas for fifteen years, from the time of the Mexican Revolution until the time of the Texas Revolution. The Mexicans had lived under Spanish rule for about 300 years. That is why they were Catholic and spoke Spanish.

During the time that Mexico ruled Texas, the law said that no Protestant churches could be formed there. So, all Christmas celebrations were Catholic services.

Many Americans moved to Texas during this time. One of them went back to Illinois and started a Protestant church. Then he brought all thirty-six members back to Texas. He did this to get around the law which did not allow any Protestant churches to be formed in Texas. He held the first legal Protestant Christmas service in Texas in 1834. It took place in Bastrop County.

An American named Joel Poinsett was sent to Mexico to buy Texas for the United States. He discovered what the Mexicans called "The Flower of Christmas Eve" and took some back to the United States. The flower became very popular as a Christmas symbol and is now

13

called the "poinsettia" in his honor. Poinsettias grow well in the Rio Grande Valley of South Texas.

Times were hard for the Americans who came to Texas. For Christmas dinner they were thankful for food like eggnog, fresh milk, and hominy.

During Mexican rule, almost 600 Scottish families settled in Central Texas. They blended in with the Americans because they spoke English. But they brought their own Christmas customs from Scotland.

For example, a Scottish tradition is that the fire in the fireplace must not go out on Christmas Eve or ghosts will come down the chimney to dance in the ashes. After celebrating Christmas, people from Scotland clean their homes spotlessly for New Year's Eve, which they call *Hogmanay*.

During the days of Mexican rule, the Americans and some of the Mexicans who lived in Texas didn't like the strict laws that the government placed on them. So they fought Mexico and won a war for freedom called the Texas Revolution. Texas became its own free country.

Throughout the state, the language and customs of Mexico are still alive. A Mexican Texan favorite for Christmas dinner and celebrations is tamales. Tamales are meat (beef, pork, or chicken) made into a paste with masa (corn flour), and then rolled inside corn shucks. The flavor can range from mild to very spicy. The corn shucks hold the tamales together, but they are not eaten.

Some Mexican families replace their porch light with a red bulb at Christmastime. The red bulb stands for the Star of Bethlehem and means that visitors are welcome. Friends come in for Christmas snacks and to see the *navidad*. The *navidad* scene is all set up, but Baby Jesus is not placed in the manger until midnight on Christmas Eve.

Another favorite tradition of Mexican Texans and

others of the Catholic religion is Midnight Mass. Mexican Texans at these church services often hear mariachi music and carols sung in both English and Spanish.

In Texas, especially along the border with Mexico, Spanish is still spoken and Catholic traditions are still followed by those of Mexican descent.

*These San Antonio girls are shown with their
Christmas tree and presents in 1902.*
— Photo courtesy University of Texas Institute of
Texan Cultures, San Antonio, Texas

16

Chapter 6

Christmas When Texas Was a Republic, 1836–1845

Texans were thrilled when the Texas Revolution earned them their freedom from Mexico. For nine years afterward, Texas was its own nation, with its own presidents.

One thing Texans were happy about was that the Mexican government could no longer require them to be Catholic. Most of the Texans were Protestants. They had come from the southern United States and spoke English. Christmas in Texas started to be celebrated outside of church, as well as in the traditional church services.

Outside of church, Texans celebrated by having dinners, dances, and parties. Friends and families gathered for singing and feasting that lasted from Christmas Eve to New Year's Day. The dances were called balls, germans, or hops. They usually had a fiddler and a square dance caller. It was a tradition to dance out the old year and dance in the new year.

Since Texas was a new nation, it was very poor. During most of the Christmases of the Republic days, eggs for eggnog and candles for decorating were too expensive for most people to buy. And sugar for cookies and cake was almost impossible to get.

During the years of the Republic, a great number of Germans came to settle in Texas. They brought with them many of the customs that Texans enjoy today.

One custom that the Germans brought to Texas in the 1840s is very popular now. In fact, most Texans wouldn't want to celebrate Christmas without a Christmas tree.

But how did it happen that the birth of Christ is celebrated by decorating a tree? It all started in Germany back in the 1300s. Most people couldn't read, so they went to plays to learn about Bible stories. On December 24, they celebrated the feast of Adam and Eve with a play.

In the Bible, Adam and Eve are the first people God created. God made for them a lovely garden and said they could eat anything they wanted except for the fruit from a certain tree. But a snake tricked Eve into eating the fruit, so she and Adam were forced to leave the garden and live with hardship from then on. This forbidden tree is usually shown as an apple tree.

In the play, the only prop on the stage was a tree they called the Paradise Tree. It was supposed to be an apple tree, but apple trees don't have any leaves in winter. So the actors would use a fir tree and hang apples on it.

Soon German people began putting Paradise Trees in their homes. This tradition continued at Christmastime, even after the plays were no longer being performed.

Gradually, the trees became more associated with Christmas than with Adam and Eve's feast day. The German people added more decorations: roses for the Virgin Mary and communion wafers for Christ. They started calling the decorated trees *"Christbaum,"* or Christ trees.

Over the years the Christmas trees grew in popularity and spread from Germany. However, in Germany the trees were placed on top of a table. Having a big floor-to-ceiling Christmas tree is a purely American tradition.

A big difference between the Christmas trees of the 1800s and our trees today is the placing of gifts. Back then the children's gifts were tied to the branches of the tree. But in the early 1900s, Americans started placing the gifts under the tree instead.

Some people didn't like the idea of decorating a tree to worship Christ. But the German Texans brought a legend to explain it. They said that when Baby Jesus was born, even trees made the journey to see him. The spruce tree traveled the farthest and was the ugliest of the trees. But then stars dropped from the sky and decorated its branches. The Star of Bethlehem landed on the very top. Baby Jesus laughed with delight at the newly decorated tree.

The legend says that parents have decorated Christmas trees ever since to make their own children laugh, as a way of worshiping Baby Jesus. Many people still put a star on the very top of the tree, to symbolize the Star of Bethlehem. Other people put an angel on top for the angels who watched over Baby Jesus and the shepherds.

In 1844 German immigrants in Texas had the first public Christmas tree. It was a big oak tree in Port Lavaca. They decorated it with candles and with the children's Christmas gifts.

By the 1850s, many Texans enjoyed having Christmas trees in their homes. This was especially true around the German settlements of New Braunfels, Gruene, and Fredericksburg. The Germans had used spruce and fir for their Christmas trees. But in Texas, they had to switch to cedar or juniper, because those were more available.

By the 1880s, Christmas trees were all the rage. People coming to Texas from Germany during the 1800s even brought the first artificial trees to Texas. They were made out of wood and the branches were turkey feathers that had been died green.

Candles began to be used on trees to symbolize Christ as the light of the world. The idea was, the more candles the better. However, this created quite a fire hazard. Today's electric Christmas tree lights are much safer.

In most Texas homes, the tree-trimming party was a family affair. But in some Czech Texan and Wendish Texan homes, the tree was left bare until Christmas Eve. Then the adults would decorate the tree behind locked doors and surprise the children with its beautiful change.

In addition to bringing Texas the Christmas tree, German Texans also brought along a song about Christmas trees, called "O Tannenbaum." The other favorite carol they brought from Germany was "Silent Night."

Red and green decorations were being used in Republic days like they are today. Red represented blood, which meant family, and green represented the hope brought by Baby Jesus.

Santa and his reindeer were not well known in Texas at this time, although he was already popular in the United States.

The Republic of Texas custom of welcoming Christmas by making noise can also be traced to an old German tradition. That tradition is called "shooting in Christmas." Men would ride about on horseback, shooting guns into the air on Christmas Eve.

There were other ways to make noise as well. Texans would pour gunpowder into holes in logs, tree stumps, or anvils and set it off. They would also fire rifles or pistols from their porches. Sometimes they would parade around blowing tin horns or beating on tin pans. The noisemaking was especially done at midnight on Christmas Eve and New Year's Eve.

All the shooting eventually led to the idea of having turkey shoots and wild game hunts. Then the noisemaking would perhaps lead to something good to eat for Christmas dinner.

There were not many toys for children during the Republic days. Children were very happy to receive apples and oranges and nuts because these were treats they couldn't get very often. When they did get toys, the toys were usually small and homemade by their parents. Girls often received cornshuck dolls or rag dolls, while boys might receive a whittled toy.

During the Christmas season in 1845, the Republic of Texas became one of the United States of America. It was a bittersweet day when Texas President Anson Jones lowered the Lone Star flag and said, "The Republic of Texas is no more."

Texas became the twenty-eighth star on the Stars and Stripes of the United States. Most Texans were glad for Texas to become a state and have the protection of the American government. But Texas was a state with a particularly proud past as its own nation.

*Father Christmas strolls the streets
at Dickens on the Strand in Galveston.*
— Photo by Elizabeth Dearing Morgan

Chapter 7

Christmas After Texas Became a State, 1845–1861

As one of the United States, Texas remained a land where most of the people were English-speaking Protestants. The sixteen years before the Civil War is called Texas' antebellum period. (*Ante* means before, and *bellum* means war.)

During Texas' antebellum statehood, Americans poured into Texas from Louisiana, Arkansas, and other states. It is from these Americans that Texas got one of its favorite Christmas characters. The Americans brought Santa Claus.

The tradition of Santa Claus started in New York City, which was settled by the Dutch and the British. Dutch children received presents from Saint Nicholas, a man who lived in the fourth century in Turkey. He was a bishop (high-ranking church official) who was known for being generous. He gave gifts to poor children. The date of his death, December 6, is known as Saint Nicholas Day. Some Texans, especially Czech Texans and Polish Texans, celebrate Saint Nicholas Day with feasting and gift-giving.

British children, on the other hand, received presents from Father Christmas. Father Christmas started delivering gifts in England when the Protestant religion was formed in the 1500s. Many Protestants did not wish to worship saints, such as Saint Nicholas. So Father Christmas, who was not a religious figure, began bringing the gifts instead.

After years of blending in New York City, the Dutch Saint Nicholas and the English Father Christmas blended into one man: the American Santa Claus. His name came from the way American children pronounced "Saint Nicholas." In 1783 he was already popular in New York City. But it would be many years before Santa made his way to most of Texas.

The image of Saint Nicholas that the Europeans brought to America was thin and serious. But in America, Santa Claus became fat and jolly, mainly because of one poem. In 1822 Clement Moore wrote the poem called "A Visit from Saint Nicholas." It starts off *"Twas the night before Christmas,"* and that is what most people call it.

In the poem, Saint Nick is described in the way that Americans have come to think of him:

> His eyes how they twinkled! His dimples how merry!
> His cheeks were like roses, his nose like a cherry.
> He had a broad face and a little round belly
> That shook, when he laughed, like a bowl full of jelly.
> He was chubby and plump, a right jolly old elf.
> And I laughed when I saw him, in spite of myself.

Although the poem never uses the words "Santa Claus," this Saint Nicholas and the American Santa Claus are the same.

The year before this poem was written, another poem was published in a magazine that described Santa Claus as driving a sleigh pulled by one reindeer. But in the Clement Moore poem, Santa Claus became the driver

24

Name: D'Andrea Tellez

SIM CIT

SECTION - I

Fill in the blank with the correct letter that match
city with the solutions.

PROBLEMS

1.) __G__ **Pollution**	
2.) __C__ **Traffic Jams**	
3.) __F__ **Crime**	
4.) __D__ **Fires**	
5.) __H__	

of a sleigh pulled by eight reindeer. All the reindeer are called by name except Rudolph, who joined Santa a hundred years later:

> When, what to my wondering eyes should appear,
> But a miniature sleigh, and eight tiny reindeer;
> "Now, Dasher! Now, Dancer! Now, Prancer! And Vixen!
> On, Comet! On, Cupid! On, Donder and Blitzen!"

The poem mentions our custom of hanging stockings for Christmas Eve:

> 'Twas the night before Christmas when all through the house
> Not a creature was stirring, not even a mouse.
> The stockings were hung by the chimney with care,
> In hopes that Saint Nicholas soon would be there.

The custom of hanging stockings for Santa to fill comes from an old legend about Saint Nicholas. He took pity on a poor family that was too proud to accept his charity. There were three daughters, and they had washed their stockings and set them by the fire to dry.

Saint Nicholas knew they would give back his money if he offered it to them. So he secretly climbed on the roof and threw gold coins down their chimney. The coins landed in the girls' stockings. The money saved the family. And to this day, children expect Saint Nick, or Santa Claus, to likewise fill their stockings when they leave them out on Christmas Eve.

In antebellum days, the stockings were socks that the children actually wore. Today the stockings are specially made for Christmas and hold lots more "stocking stuffers."

"A Visit from Saint Nicholas" was printed in newspapers after it was written. But in 1848 it was first published as a separate book with illustrations. By 1860 it was the best known Christmas poem in the United States and had made its way to Texas, as well.

In addition to "A Visit from Saint Nicholas," another great Christmas story came to Texas during its antebellum statehood days. *A Christmas Carol* was written in England by Charles Dickens in 1843. It became popular in England immediately and then in America and Texas a few years later.

A Christmas Carol features the characters Bob Cratchit, his son Tiny Tim, and Ebenezer Scrooge, who learns a lesson about being generous from the Ghosts of Christmas Past, Christmas Present, and Christmas Yet-to-Come.

A Christmas Carol has been made into many movies and cartoons. During the month of December, it is also performed as a play in many towns throughout Texas.

There are two Texas Christmas festivals that honor Charles Dickens for writing *A Christmas Carol*. Dickens on the Strand is a weekend-long event that includes the Christmas festivities of good eating, good shopping, and good entertainment. The Galveston Historical Foundation transforms eight blocks of the historic downtown Galveston business district into an 1857 London Christmas scene. The Strand is famous for its Victorian buildings. (Victorian refers to the period 1837–1901, when Queen Victoria ruled England.)

All of the entertainers, food vendors, gift sellers, and even policemen are dressed in Victorian costumes. More than 200 merchants sell Victorian-style Christmas presents and British food and drink. ("British" refers to England, Scotland, and Wales.) Artists sell handmade gifts like cloth dolls and teddy bears, china dolls and tea sets, doll clothes, wooden toys and guns, and Christmas ornaments. There is face painting and also a Victorian carousel to ride.

British snacks that you're not likely to find many other places in Texas are Scotch eggs and plum pudding. Scotch eggs are hard-boiled, wrapped in sausage, battered, breaded, and deep fried. Plum pudding is a tradi-

The ghost of Scrooge's old business partner, Jacob Marley, rattles his chains in the Queen's Parade at Dickens on the Strand.
— Photo by Jim Cruz

tional Victorian English food. It is steamed four hours and then topped with brandy and brandied hard sauce.

If your Christmas cards are ready to mail, you can mail them at the Dickens Postal Station. There they will be stamped with a special Dickens postmark.

The highlight of Dickens on the Strand is the Queen's Parade. It features characters from Dickens' books, bagpipers, and Victorian ladies and gentlemen.

The other festival honoring the English writer is called Dickens in the Park in Farmers Branch. Like Galveston's Strand, Farmers Branch Historical Park is transformed to nineteenth-century London. There are horse-drawn carriage rides, tours of historic homes, costumed carolers and musicians, readings from Dickens' novels, and scenes from *A Christmas Carol*.

An English custom that Charles Dickens wrote about is kissing under the mistletoe. Mistletoe is an evergreen plant with white berries. It grows on the highest branches of trees, never touching the ground. That's why it's considered unlucky to ever let mistletoe touch the ground.

Mistletoe has been very special to the British since before the days of Christ. They thought that mistletoe would ensure that many children would be born. That may be where the custom of kissing under the mistletoe came from.

The English Texans were very happy to find lots of mistletoe growing in the trees of Texas. They hung mistletoe "kissing boughs" over doorways. Any girl who was caught under the mistletoe could not refuse a kiss. If she did, she supposedly would not be married in the coming year.

In the olden days, a berry was plucked off each time someone was kissed. When all the berries were gone, the kissing stopped. Today people usually leave the berries on so the fun can continue. Central Texas produces most of the mistletoe for the whole world.

An English Texan holds up a fistful of mistletoe for sale at Dickens on the Strand in Galveston.

— Photo by Nancy Dearing Johnson

29

Another Christmas plant is holly. It has prickly leaves and red berries. The British decorated with this evergreen plant in the winter long before there was such a thing as Christmas. But when the Christmas celebration began, the British made a legend about holly and how it symbolized Christ's death on the cross. They said the prickly leaves stood for his crown of thorns, and the red berries stood for drops of his blood. There is even a Christmas carol that says, "Of all the trees that are in the wood the holly bears the crown."

English Texans were glad to find that two varieties of holly grew in Texas. Yaupon holly and possumhaw holly both produce red berries that birds love to eat. If you plant Texas holly in your yard, you will have planted a pretty, easy-to-care-for feast for birds to eat at Christmastime. And a sprig of holly on the bedpost is supposed to bring happy dreams.

Another British custom that was widely practiced in Texas during the 1800s is the burning of the yule log. The yule log is a huge oak log placed at the back of the parlor fireplace. A fire of smaller logs in front of it gradually burns it away. The holidays lasted as long as the yule log still burned, which was supposed to be Christmas to New Year's.

While the British Texans drank their wassail punch and burned their yule logs, the German Texans in New Braunfels celebrated antebellum statehood Christmases with aniseed cakes and cedar trees. The trees were lighted with homemade tallow candles. Friends would gather around and decorate the tree with pieces of glass, metal, and cotton; cookies and candies; and red berries, moss, mistletoe, and greenery. They also decorated the tree with fruits such as apples, and nuts such as pecans, which they would wrap in colored cloth or paper. Popcorn and red peppers were made into long garlands and strung around the tree.

Children usually received homemade gifts like toy wagons or willow whistles for boys and rag or cornhusk dolls for girls. In the larger cities like San Antonio, children from families who had plenty of money might receive store-bought toys, such as china dolls or rocking horses. Stockings were filled with fruit, candy, and nuts. If the kids were lucky, they might find a dime in the toe of the stocking.

Christmas gifts were mainly for children. If teenagers or adults got any gifts, they were usually knitted socks, mittens, scarves, or caps, and some candies.

Following Texas' frontier heritage, Christmas was still a rowdy time. After church services, people liked to set off fireworks. Sometimes men still formed noisy parades by going from house to house blowing on tin horns and beating on tin pans. They would demand that the men of each house join them in their noisemaking.

Feasting was an important part of Christmas in Texas, and the cooking was mostly done over a fireplace. Christmas favorites were roasted wild turkey, roasted kid *(cabrito)*, tamales, and eggnog.

Upper-class people in the big cities held masquerade balls and confetti carnivals for Christmas. The people would dress up in costumes for an elegant evening of dancing, or for a parade on horseback.

Christmas of 1860 was the last to be celebrated in antebellum Texas. Early in 1861, Texas seceded from, or left, the United States of America. Texas joined the other Southern states in forming a new nation called the Confederate States of America.

Chapter 8

Christmas When Texas Was a Confederate State, 1861–1865

The Confederate States of America was a nation made up of eleven Southern states: Virginia, North Carolina, South Carolina, Tennessee, Georgia, Alabama, Florida, Mississippi, Louisiana, Arkansas, and Texas. The entire four years that the Confederate States of America existed, it was embroiled in a war with the United States of America. This war, the American Civil War, is often called the War Between the States by those in the South.

The people in the South felt that they were not being represented by the government of the United States. That is why they formed their own government. Just like the Americans fought the British for their freedom in the American Revolution, the Confederates fought the Union for their freedom in the War Between the States.

Although the South was badly outnumbered and had no factories to make guns and supplies like the North did, the farmers of the South fought valiantly for four years before the North could claim victory. These four years were a bittersweet time for the South. The

Confederates were very proud that they had their own country. But the war took its toll. Many people were killed and many homes and farms in the South were destroyed. The war also caused shortages of food, medicine, clothing, and other supplies.

The people in Confederate Texas had to celebrate Christmas with the same self-sufficiency that had won them the Texas Revolution. Everything they ate, wore, and gave as gifts was homemade. The shortages made it difficult for Santa to do much for the Southern boys and girls. But they usually got to pop off gunpowder and attend services in a decorated church. As under the United States, most Confederate Texans were English-speaking Protestants.

The shortages also made it difficult to do the Christmas baking because there was no sugar or raisins. Few items were available for sale, and what was for sale was outrageously expensive. And most people didn't have much money. Families would gather what they could and send it to their men who were in battle. Favorite items to send were smoked meats, warm clothing, and tobacco.

Self-sufficiency grew more important each year that the war drug on. The people of Confederate Texas had to make not only their own clothes, but also their own coats and shoes.

Texans did what they could at Christmas. The wealthier ones had cedar Christmas trees with homemade gifts tied to the branches. The trees were also decorated with popcorn garlands and little cornucopias ("horns of plenty" made from rolled-up paper) filled with nuts and candies. Those who could get it drank eggnog.

A Confederate Christmas is celebrated each year in Dallas. It is hosted by the Dallas area United Daughters of the Confederacy. The guests dress in Confederate-style clothing and enjoy a Southern dinner and music. They can even have their Christmas photos taken with an actor dressed up as Confederate General Robert E. Lee.

The United Daughters of the Confederacy are women whose ancestors fought for the South during the War Between the States. The money they raise from A Confederate Christmas is used to restore the Confederate Monument at Pioneer Park in downtown Dallas. The Confederate Monument was placed there in 1896.

The Confederates were finally defeated after a heroic four-year effort. Texas became one of the United States again. But the Southern traditions are still alive in Texas, especially near the borders Texas shares with two other former Confederate states, Louisiana and Arkansas.

Chapter 9

Christmas in Texas
After the Civil War, 1865–Present

When the War Between the States ended, the Confederacy was no more. The eleven states that formed the Confederacy, including Texas, once again became part of the United States of America. As had been the case since the Republic days of 1836, most Texans were Protestant and spoke English.

The former Confederate states went through a tough time after the war. It was called Reconstruction. The United States government sent troops to the South to be sure that U.S. laws were being obeyed. There were hard feelings between the Confederate Texans and the United States. But, as more than 130 years have passed, Texas again is proud to be a part of the United States.

Reconstruction was even more severe in the other Southern states. Many Southerners came to Texas to start a new life. With them they brought American Christmas traditions, such as the Christmas card. These became popular in America, and then Texas, in the 1880s. They had started out in England in the 1840s, copying the already popular Valentine cards.

It wasn't until 1907 that Christmas seals were sold in America. They are used as stickers to seal the Christmas card envelopes. Christmas seals are sold to raise money for charity. The idea came from Denmark.

In the 1870s, Texas Rangers (the state police) often found themselves far from home at Christmas. Luckily, Texas has plenty of wildlife. A Ranger with a rifle was able to hunt a good meal back then. Popular main dishes were turkey, deer, geese, and duck. They also ate other animals that most people today would not consider eating, such as buffalo, antelope, and bear.

For dessert there might be ice cream (milk and vanilla set outside to freeze) or fruitcake.

Texas is famous for fruitcake. In 1896, a German baker opened the Collin Street Bakery in Corsicana (south of Dallas). He used his German recipe to make DeLuxe fruitcakes. One hundred years later, the Collin Street Bakery still uses this recipe to make fruitcakes that are placed in holiday tins and mailed around the world. DeLuxe fruitcakes are made of pecans, honey, cherries, and pineapples, and are decorated by hand.

Other Texans far from home at Christmastime were the United States soldiers who fought Indians. Fort Concho was founded near San Angelo in 1867. Throughout the 1870s, there were delightful Christmas parties, dances, dinners, and church services. The parties featured a Christmas tree with Santa giving gifts. The dinners featured turkey, ham, and cakes for dessert. The church was decorated with evergreens and mistletoe.

The United States soldiers left Fort Concho in 1889. But today, the fort has been restored. Now Christmas at Old Fort Concho offers an enjoyable look at life at the fort in the 1800s, with good food and good entertainment for the visitors.

There are also Christmas celebrations at Old Fort

This enormous Christmas tree decorates the Texas State Capitol rotunda in Austin.
— Photo courtesy *Texas Highways* Magazine

Croghan in Burnet, decorated as in the year 1849, and Fort Davis National Historical Site in Fort Davis.

The year 1879 was an important one for Christmas in Texas. That was the first year for Christmas to be an official state holiday.

Before, during, and after the War Between the States, an American artist named Thomas Nast had been drawing pictures and cartoons of Santa Claus for magazines and books. It was through his drawings that Santa gradually became less like an elf and more like a fat, jolly human. Instead Santa began to have elves who lived with him and helped him make all the toys.

No one knew where Santa lived and worked until 1882, when Nast drew Santa's workshop at the North Pole. The North Pole was also in the news that year because explorers from different countries were trying to be the first to reach it.

A good number of Italians began coming to Texas at this time. A popular tradition that began in Italy is the Nativity scene. Saint Francis of Assisi made the first Nativity scene in 1223, using statues and live animals. The idea spread to churches, and then to homes. By the time most Italians arrived in Texas, the popularity of Nativity scenes had long since spread throughout Europe and America. Most manger scenes have Mary, Joseph, Baby Jesus, the Three Wise Men, shepherds, angels, sheep, and cattle. Some have shepherds offering gifts from Texas.

Cowboys in Texas celebrated Christmas on their ranches with horse races and tournaments on horseback. The men would compete with lances like the knights of olden days in England. The winners would be honored at a Christmas Eve ball.

One tradition that started during this time was the Texas Cowboys' Christmas Ball in Anson, a small town near Abilene in West Texas. The first ball took place at the Morning Star Hotel in 1885. Cowboys and ladies danced the night away.

38

*A West Texan and his lady dance at the Cowboys' Christmas Ball
in Anson.*
— Photo by Nancy Dearing Johnson

A visitor named Larry Chittenden was there, and later he told the story of the dance in a poem. The poem, and the ball, became famous. Part of it goes like this:

> 'Way out in Western Texas, where the Clear Fork's waters flow,
> Where the cattle are "a-browzin'," an' the Spanish ponies grow;
> Where the antelope is grazin' and the lonely plovers call —
> It was there that I attended "The Cowboys' Christmas Ball."
> The town was Anson City, old Jones' county seat,
> Where they raise Polled Angus cattle, and waving whiskered wheat;
> 'Twas there, I say, at Anson, with the lively "widder Wall,"
> That I went to that reception, "The Cowboys' Christmas Ball."

The balls were temporarily stopped when the Morning Star Hotel burned down in the early 1900s. But in 1934, two schoolteachers decided to revive the tradition and held a Cowboys' Christmas Ball pageant in the high school gym. It was so popular that in 1938 people began work on a rock building that was made especially to hold the ball. Pioneer Hall was completed in 1940, and the Texas Cowboys' Christmas Ball has been held there ever since. It takes place the Thursday, Friday, and Saturday before Christmas each year.

The poem mentions by name some of the dancers who were at the original ball. Today, descendants of these cowboys return to dance at the balls each year. The building contains a huge wooden dance floor, but there are no tables. Bleachers line the sides of the dance floor for those who want a rest.

In keeping with the traditions of the first ball of 1885, women are required to wear dresses and men are required to go without a hat. Almost everyone wears cowboy boots, and many men wear knee-high boots with their pants tucked in, as the original cowboys did. Many women wear long, full dresses of the style of the ladies of 1885, while others wear modern-day western skirts and blouses.

Between 1890 and 1920 a large number of Greeks came to Texas. Most Greeks are members of the Orthodox church, the smallest group of Christians in Texas. Greek Texans usually go to church on Christmas Day. Then they go home and eat a cesnica cake. It has a silver coin baked inside it. Whoever gets the piece with the coin will have good luck.

Orthodox Texans like to use straw in their Christmas wreaths and decorations. It reminds them of the stable where Baby Jesus was born. They may spread straw around the Christmas tree or around the center of the table.

During the 1800s, Americans brought many Christmas carols into Texas. Some of the popular ones are "We Three Kings of Orient Are," "O Little Town of Bethlehem," and "It Came Upon the Midnight Clear." A Texas author, O. Henry, wrote a Christmas story called "The Gift of the Magi." Magi is what some people call the Three Wise Men.

American songwriters introduced two more beloved Christmas characters to Texas. "Rudolph the Red-Nosed Reindeer" started out as a book in 1939, a popular song in 1949, and a television movie in 1964. As the song says,

Rudolph the Red-Nosed Reindeer had a very shiny nose
And if you ever saw it, you would even say it glows.

Although the other reindeer laughed at Rudolph's nose and called him names, Rudolph earned their respect by saving Christmas.

"Frosty the Snowman" was the other famous character, born as a song in 1950. Then he was featured in books and a television movie. Other great Christmas carols written by Americans during this time were "Jingle Bells," "Santa Claus is Coming to Town," "Up on the Housetop," and "White Christmas."

As the years progressed, Christmas trees and Santa

Claus became more and more popular in Texas. During the 1900s, many Texas cities began to put up a city Christmas tree. Also, Santa Claus took a fat, jolly woman to be his wife. Her name is Mrs. Claus.

Texans are lucky to have the Mary Elizabeth Hopkins Santa Claus Museum in their state. Mary Elizabeth Hopkins collected over 2,000 figures of Santa during her lifetime (1913–1990). When she died, her family decided to share her treasures with the public by opening the Santa Claus Museum.

The museum is in a cottage on the grounds of the Dilue Rose Harris House Museum in Columbus, Texas. It is open year-round, but there is a special open house on the first day of Columbus' Christmas on the Colorado celebration (usually the first weekend in December).

Although evergreen and mistletoe still decorate homes and churches, the invention of electric bulbs meant that candles weren't the only way to light up the holidays. And Texans continued to dance and dine and sing their way through Christmas.

Chapter 10

Texas Christmas Celebrations Today

In every town in Texas, large or small, you are likely to find a Christmas celebration. Especially popular are community Christmas tree lightings and Christmas parades. Holiday home tours and open houses are also very popular.

In many towns there are driving tours or hayrides, special Christmas arts and crafts shopping events, Christmas walks, concerts, caroling, parties, and services. There are also many Christmas pageants, plays, balls, and exhibits.

As an example of how popular Christmas tree lightings are, the Texas State Museum of History in Arlington hosts a Victorian Christmas and the City of Arlington Christmas Tree Lighting Ceremony at the Fielder House.

There is a Christmas Bird Count or census at the Aransas National Wildlife Refuge in Austwell/Tivoli.

Throughout the state there are also Renaissance Christmas celebrations and madrigal dinners. Amusement parks even get into the spirit. Fiesta Texas in San

Antonio hosts a Lone Star Christmas and Six Flags in Arlington hosts Holiday in the Park.

Here are some additional Texas Christmas celebrations.

CHRISTMAS ON THE CORRIDOR

On the first Saturday in December, Pony Express couriers ride like the wind to deliver Christmas greetings from the governor. Starting in Goliad, the riders take three different routes through the Alamo-LaBahia corridor. The corridor is about ninety miles long and is named for missions in San Antonio and Goliad.

Each town on the Pony Express routes celebrates the day with special Christmas shopping, good eating, and Christmas music. Each town may celebrate a little differently, but there are often historical tours, church services, visits from Santa, and Las Posadas. Some people like to stay all day at one town's celebration, while others like to follow the Pony Express routes and visit several towns.

Most of the Christmas on the Corridor towns stretch along the San Antonio River or Cibolo Creek. They are Goliad, Runge, Kenedy, Helena, Panna Maria, Karnes City, Hobson, Falls City, Cestohowa, Poth, Floresville, Stockdale, Sutherland Springs, Pleasanton, Elmendorf, La Vernia, Saint Hedwig, and the final stop on the Pony Express route: San Antonio.

HILL COUNTRY REGIONAL LIGHTING TOUR

The Hill Country Regional Lighting Tour shows off the lights in several Central Texas towns: Blanco, Burnet, Boerne, Bulverde, Johnson City, Lampasas, Marble Falls, Mason, Round Mountain, Fredericksburg, and Llano.

The towns are ablaze with thousands of lights. Oftentime the county courthouse is one of the most decorated buildings. Besides the spectacular lights, each community holds other Christmas events as well. These might include a parade, tour of historic buildings, special shopping, or Las Posadas.

STATE PARKS

Christmas events take place at several Texas state parks. Christmas at Goliad State Park (Goliad, Texas) includes a play at the mission. After the play the mission is lit up, and there is a live Nativity, *piñatas,* and Mexican hot chocolate.

At Eisenhower State Park in Denison, guests celebrate Christmas Valley in Cedar Hollow with Christmas music, lights, and displays.

Norwegian Christmas in the Park takes place at Meridian State Park (Meridian, Texas). Norwegian Christmas traditions are followed, including food, costumes, decorations, and entertainment.

In La Grange, a Kreische Christmas is celebrated at the Kreische Home in Monument Hill State Park. They celebrate with 1860s German-style costumes, decorations, choirs, and dulcimer music.

A Christmas Open House and Las Posadas at the Lodge both take place at the Indian Lodge in Davis Mountains State Park. The open house includes choirs, baked goods, and a gingerbread village. Davis Mountains State Park is located in Fort Davis, Texas.

STATE HISTORICAL PARKS

There are also Christmas celebrations at historical parks throughout the state. These include Cowboy Christmas at Varner-Hogg Plantation State Historical Park in West Columbia. There are tours of the plantation and barn, pony rides, roping and branding lessons for children, a chuck wagon supper, tall tales around the campfire, caroling, and the lighting of the park's 40,000 Christmas lights.

*These people are celebrating Christmas in Goliad as it was
celebrated in the Texas Republic days.*
— Photo courtesy *Texas Highways* Magazine

In Washington, 'Twas a Nineteenth Century Christmas is celebrated at Washington-on-the-Brazos State Historical Park.

The Maxey House Christmas Gala takes place at Sam Bell Maxey House State Historical Park in Paris.

In Seguin, A Taste of Christmas Past is celebrated at Sebastopol House State Historical Park.

And in Stonewall, the Christmas Tree Lighting at LBJ State Historical Park includes a tour of the park and live Nativity, in addition to the lighting of the native cedar Christmas tree.

CHRISTMAS LIGHTS AND PARADES

Many towns in Texas have light displays for people to drive or walk through. In Del Rio, it is called the Festival of Lights. In Marshall, it is called the Wonderland of Lights. It only started in 1987, but the Wonderland of Lights has already become the nation's largest holiday light show. More than four and a half million lights are used!

Parades are another way many Texas towns celebrate Christmas. Probably the largest one in Texas is the Adolphus/Children's Christmas Parade in Dallas. It is featured on national television. The parade raises money for Children's Medical Center of Dallas.

No matter where you go in Texas, you are likely to find a meaningful, enjoyable, rewarding way to celebrate Christmas.

Marty Kaderli makes Christmas tree cookies on a wood-burning stove at LBJ State Historical Park.
— Photo courtesy *Texas Highways* Magazine

For
information
about Texas
Christmas events,
call the
Texas Department of
Transportation's travel number:
1-800-452-9292.
You can also write them to get
a calendar of Texas
Christmas events that
will take place in December.

The address is:
Texas Events Calendar, P.O. Box 5064, Austin, TX 78763.

SPAIN   FRANCE   MEXICO

TEXAS   CONFEDERACY   UNITED STATES

Bibliography

Albright, Dawn. *Texas Festivals.* El Campo: Palmetto Press, 1991.

Alter, Judy, and Joyce Gibson Roach, editors. *Texas and Christmas: A Collection of Traditions, Memories, and Folklore.* Fort Worth: Texas Christian University Press, 1983.

Barth, Edna. *Holly, Reindeer, and Colored Lights: The Story of the Christmas Symbols.* New York: The Seabury Press, 1971.

Bedford, Annie North, retold by. *Frosty the Snow Man.* Adapted from the song of the same name (1950). New York: Golden Book, 1989.

Gardner, Horace J. *Let's Celebrate Christmas.* New York: The Ronald Press Company, 1940, 1950, 1968.

Giblin, James Cross. *The Truth About Santa Claus.* New York: Thomas Y. Crowell, 1985.

Hazen, Barbara Shook. *Rudolph the Red-nosed Reindeer.* Racine, Wisconsin: Golden Press, 1976. (Adapted from the 1958 story by Robert L. May.)

The Holy Bible, King James Version. Philadelphia: The National Bible Press, 1611, 1963 printing.

Miles, Clement A. *Christmas Customs and Traditions: Their History and Significance.* New York: Dover Publications, 1976. (Originally published as *Christmas in Ritual and Tradition, Christian and Pagan* by T. Fisher Unwin in 1912.)

Moore, Clement C. *The Night Before Christmas.* Racine, Wisconsin: Golden Press, 1822, 1949, 1977.

Ruff, Ann. *The Best of Texas Festivals: Your Guide to Rootin'*

Tootin' Downhome Texas Good Times. Houston: Lone Star Books, 1986.

Silverthorne, Elizabeth. *Christmas in Texas.* College Station: Texas A&M University Press, 1990 (second printing, 1993).

Snyder, Phillip V. *The Christmas Tree Book: The History of the Christmas Tree and Antique Christmas Tree Ornaments.* New York: Penguin Books, 1976, 1977 (1983 printing).

———. *December 25th: The Joys of Christmas Past.* New York: Dodd, Mead & Company, 1985.

Stevens, Patricia Bunning. *Merry Christmas! A History of the Holiday.* New York: Macmillan Publishing Company, 1979.

Wernecke, Herbert H. *Christmas Customs Around the World.* Philadelphia: The Westminster Press, 1959.

Acknowledgments

Thanks to the following family members who helped with travel plans for this book: my sister Nancy Dearing Johnson, her husband Louis Johnson, their sons Jason and Justin Johnson; my son Clint Morgan, his father Tom Morgan; my brother and sister-in-law Clyde and Tamra Dearing, their son Travis Dearing; and my parents, Jo Anne and Olin Dearing.

Thanks for help with photographs goes to photo-illustrator Nancy Dearing Johnson; to photo archivist Tom Shelton and librarian Diane Bruce at the University of Texas Institute of Texan Cultures at San Antonio; and to David Bush, public relations/marketing director at the Galveston Historical Foundation.

Index

55

About the Author

ELIZABETH DEARING MORGAN

Elizabeth Dearing Morgan has celebrated each of her "more than thirty" Christmases in Texas. All four of her grandparents were born in Texas, and all eight of her great-grandparents lived and died in Texas.

Elizabeth is an eighth-generation Texan and member of the Daughters of the Republic of Texas, a tenth-generation Southerner and member of the United Daughters of the Confederacy, and an eleventh-generation American and member of the Daughters of the American Revolution.

Her previous books published by Eakin Press are *President Mirabeau B. Lamar: Father of Texas Education,* a pho-tobiography for children; and *Jane Long: A Child's Pictorial History,* a photobiography of the Mother of Texas.

Elizabeth is a Texas secondary schoolteacher, certified in social studies, reading, English, business, and home economics. She lives in Austin and offers programs for adults and children. Contact the publisher at 512/288-1771 for author visits.